A Narrative of the Life and Travels of Mrs. Nancy Prince

A Narrative of the Life and Travels of Mrs. Nancy Prince

Nancy Prince

MINT EDITIONS

A Narrative of the Life and Travels of Mrs. Nancy Prince was first published in 1850.

This edition published by Mint Editions 2020.

ISBN 9781513278643 | E-ISBN 9781513279107

Published by Mint Editions®

MINT EDITIONS

minteditionbooks.com

Publishing Director: Jennifer Newens
Design & Production: Rachel Lopez Metzger
Project Manager: Micaela Clark
Typesetting: Westchester Publishing Services

Narrative

As my unprofitable life has been spared, and I have been, by the providence of God, wonderfully preserved, it is with gratitude to my Heavenly Father, and duty to myself, that I attempt to give to the public a short narrative of my life and travels.

I was born in Newburyport, in 1799. My mother was the daughter of Tobias Wornton, who was stolen from Africa, when a lad, and was a slave of Capt. Winthrop Sargent; and, although a slave, he fought for liberty, and was in the Revolutionary army at the battle of Bunker Hill. My grandmother was an Indian. My father, Thomas Gardener, was born on Nantucket; his parents were of African descent, and he died of bleeding at the lungs, leaving my mother a widow the second time, with an infant in her arms. She then returned to Gloucester, her native place. My mother soon married again her third husband, by whom she had six children. My step-father was stolen from Africa, and while the vessel was at anchor in one of the Eastern ports, he succeeded in making his escape from his captors by swimming ashore. After a lapse of two years he came to Gloucester, and followed the sea, and was twelve years with Capt. Elias Davis, in the employ of Capt. Fitz W. Sargent. During the war he was taken by a British Privateer, and pressed into their service. He was sick with the dropsy a long while, and died in 1813. My mother was again left a widow, with an infant six weeks old. When she heard of her husband's death, she replied, "I thought it; what shall I do with these children?" Her grief, poverty, and responsibilities, were too much for her; she never was the mother that she had been before. I was at this time in Capt. Sargent's family. I shall never forget the feelings I experienced on hearing of the decease of my father-in-law; he was never very kind to the first set of children. But by industry, a humble home was provided for my mother and younger children. Death had twice visited our family within three months, my father having buried my grandfather before he sailed. I thought I would go home a little while, and try to comfort my mother. The three oldest children were put into families. My brother and myself went out of town, in one family, where we staid until the war was over. We often went home with our wages, and all the comforts we could get; but we could not approach our mother as we wished. God in mercy took one little brother of seven years, who had pined in consumption; thus our family was scattered. I determined to get more for my labor, and I left Essex and went to Salem, in 1814, to service in a family. I had always enjoyed the happy privilege of religious instruction. My dear grandfather was a member of a Congregational Church, and a good man; he always attended church in the morning, and took us with him; and in the afternoon he took care of the smaller children, while my mother attended with her little group. He thought it wrong for us to go to a school where the teacher was not devoted to God, for I early knew the difference between right and wrong. They had family prayers morning and evening. I often looked at them, and thought to myself, "Is this your religion?" I did not wonder that the girl who had lived there previous to myself, went home to die. There were seven in the family; two of them being sick, one with a fever and the other in a consumption, of course the work must have been very severe, especially the washing. Sabbath evening I had to prepare for the wash. I was then but fourteen years of age, and a stranger. I was called up at two o'clock in the morning, and what embittered my heavy task, I was not spoken kindly to, but was blamed for being slow, and for not performing my work well. Hard labor and unkindness were too much for me, and in three months my health and strength were gone. I went home to Gloucester in their chaise. I found my mother in poor health, but through the mercy of God, and the attention and skill of Dr. Dale, and the kindness of friends, I was restored, so that in a few months I was able again to go to work, although my side afflicted me, which I attributed to over-working myself.

In 1815 I returned to Salem, accompanied by my eldest sister, and obtained good places. She afterwards returned to Boston as a nursery girl, where she lived a few months, and was deluded away on February 7th of 1815. A friend came to Salem and informed me of it. Her death would not have been so painful to me. We loved each other very much, and more particularly as our step-father was not very kind to us; we used to say as soon as we were large enough we would go away, as we did. It was very cold, but notwithstanding, I was so distressed about my sister, that I started on foot the next morning after I heard of it. At Lynn Hotel we refreshed ourselves, and all seemed much interested about me. Two women took me aside, and inquired how it was I was with that woman. I told my reason. My companion had a little son of hers in her arms. By the time we were seven miles from Salem, cold and fatigued, I could walk no farther, and we hired a horse and sleigh, and a man to drive us to Boston, where we arrived at seven in the evening. I put up with a friend of mine, who lived in Bedford street, who received me very kindly. My feet, hands, and ears, were all frost-bitten. I needed all the hospitality that was extended to me. I was young and inexperienced, but my object was hallowed. God chooses in his wisdom the weak things of earth; without his aid how could I ever have rescued my lost sister! Mr. Brown, when he learned my errand, kindly offered to assist me. He found where my sister resided, and taking with him a large cane, he accompanied me to the house. My sister I found seated, with a number of others, round a fire, the mother of harlots at the head. My sister did not see me until I clasped her round the neck. The old woman flew at me, and bid me take my hands off of her. Mr. Brown defended me with his cane from her attacks. There were many men as well as girls there, and all was confusion. When my sister came to herself, she looked upon me. I said, "Sylvia, my dear sister, what are you here for? Will you go with me?" The enraged old woman cried out, "No, she cannot go." Sylvia replied, "I will go." Then followed a scene. The old woman seized her to drag her down into the kitchen; I held on to her, while Mr. Brown, at my side, so used his great cane, and so threatened her, that she was obliged to let her go; and, after collecting her things, she left the house with Mr. Brown and myself.

The next day we started for Salem, and went to the stage-office; we expected Mr. Low, the driver of the Gloucester stage, who knew us as his towns-people, would let us take passage with him without any difficulty; but he refused, unless we would ride upon the top. It was very cold, and we had never rode in that way; his inhumanity grieves me even now. I had sent my mother my wages the week before, and what money I had, I had taken in advance of my employers. We were greatly embarrassed, when a colored man, unknown to us, penetrated our difficulties, and asked us if we had two dollars; we told him we had; he very kindly took us to another stage-office, and we bargained for a horse and sleigh to take us to Salem, where we arrived safely in about two hours and a half; and we gave up our conveyance to the same owners, with ten thousand thanks to our colored friend, and to our Heavenly Father; for had we attempted to walk, we must have frozen by the way. The lady I lived with (Mrs. John Deland,) received us very kindly, and permitted my sister to remain with me awhile; then she returned to Gloucester, to the family who brought her up, and I thought we had gained a great victory.

My brother George and myself were very desirous of making our mother comfortable; he went to sea for that purpose. The next April I came to Boston, to get a higher price for my labor, for we had agreed to maintain our mother, and we hoped she would take our little brother, who was supported by the town, and take care of him. George came home, and sailed again in the same vessel, leaving her a drawbill of half of his wages. My sister returned to Boston to find me, and wished to procure a place to work out. She tried me much. I thought it a needy time, for I had not yielded my heart to the will of God, though I had many impressions, and formed many resolutions; but the situation that I had been placed in, having left my mother's home at the age of eight, had not permitted me to do as I wished, though the kind counsels of my dear grandfather and pious teachers followed me wherever I went. Care after care oppressed me; my mother wandered about like a Jew; the young children who were in families were dissatisfied; all hope but in God was lost. I then resolved in my mind to seek an interest in my Saviour, and put my trust in him. For that purpose I changed my place for one more retired, got my sister with me, and then God blessed my soul; being justified by faith, I found peace with God, even the forgiveness of sins, through Jesus Christ. After living sixteen years and five months without any hope, myself and seven others were baptized, in obedience to the great command.

My brother George returned home, and we again provided a home for mother and the little ones; he went to sea, and affairs now seemed to promise comfort and respectability. But mother chose to marry again; this was like death to us all. George returned home, but was so disappointed, that he shipped again to come no more. Although a boy of sixteen years, he was as steady and capable as most men at twenty. My cares were consequently increased, having no one to share them with me. My next brother, who lived in S. Essex, came to Salem to his mother, but was driven away by her husband, and came to me. I carried him to Gloucester, and left him in the hands of the town; but he stayed but three weeks, and returned to me again. I then boarded him for one dollar a week, until I could procure suitable employment.

When winter came, poor mother's health was declining; little Samuel could do but little; my father-in-law was very cross, for he expected to be supported by my brother George. I could not see my mother suffer; I therefore left my place and went to Salem, to watch over her and Samuel, and lived with the Rev. Dr. Boles's family. In the spring I returned to Boston, and took my brother with me. Soon after, my sister Lucy left her place and went to her mother, but was not permitted to stay. My mother wrote to me, requesting me to take care of her. I then determined in my mind to bring her to Boston, and, if possible, procure a place for her; and on her arrival, I obtained board for her and Samuel at a friend's, for one dollar a week. My brother John, that I had boarded, at last got a place where he had wages; soon the Lord opened a way for little Samuel. Dr. Phelps took him to bring up, so that I was left with one only to sustain. Soon my hopes were blasted. John left his place, and was several months on my hands again; finally, he made up his mind to go to sea. I was so thankful that he had concluded to do something, that I took two month's wages in advance to fit him out for Liverpool. In five months he returned, without a single thing but what he stood in; his wages were small, not enough to render him comfortable; had not a friend given him a home, he would have been again dependent on my exertions. Another friend took Lucy, with whom she staid eleven months; she continued in different families for some time, till she was about twelve. I left her at the Rev. Mr. Mann's family, at Westminster, for a certain time, thinking it would be best for her, and John I left to fight his own battles. My sister Sylvia was one of my greatest trials. Knowing she was in Boston, my mother, in one of her spells of insanity, got away from her home, and travelled here after her. She came where I lived. My employers were very kind to her. After tarrying a few days with me, I hired a horse and chaise, and took them both back to Salem; and returned back to my place in 1822, with a determination to do something for myself. I left my place after three months, and went to learn a trade; and, after seven years of anxiety and toil, I made up my mind to leave this country.

September 1st, 1823, Mr. Prince arrived from Russia; February 15th, I was married; April 14th, embarked in brig Romulus, arrived at Elsinore May 24th, left the same day for Copenhagen, where we remained twelve days. We visited the King's Palace, and several other extensive and beautiful buildings. We attended a number of entertainments among the Danes and English, which were religiously observed; their manners and customs are similar; they are very attentive to strangers; the Sabbath is strictly observed; the principal religion is the Lutheran and Calvinistic, but all persuasions are tolerated. The languages of that people are Dutch, French, English, &c. The Danes are very modest and kind, but, like all other nations, they well know how to take the advantage. I left there the 7th of June, and arrived at Cronstradt on the 19th; left there the 21st for St. Petersburg, and in a few hours were happy to find ourselves at our place of destination, through the blessing of God, in good health, and soon made welcome from all quarters. We took lodgings with a Mrs. Robinson, a native of our country, who was Patience Mott, of Providence, who left there in the year 1813, in the family of Alexander Gabriel, the man who was taken for Mr. Prince. There I spent six weeks very pleasantly, visiting and receiving friends, after the manner of the country. We then commenced housekeeping. While there I attended two of their parties; there were various amusements in which I did not participate, which caused them much disappointment. I told them my religion did not allow of dancing or dice playing, which formed part of the amusements. As they were very strict in their religion, they indulged me in the same privilege. By the help of God I was ever enabled to maintain my stand.

Mr. Prince was born in Marlborough, and lived in families in this city. In 1810 he went to Gloucester, and sailed with Captain Theodore Stanwood for Russia; he returned with him, and remained in his family, and at this time visited my mother's family. He again sailed with him, in 1812, for the last time. Captain Stanwood took with him his son Theodore, for the purpose of attending school in the city of St. Petersburg. Mr. Prince went to serve Princess Purtossozof, one of the noble ladies of Court. It is well known that the color of one's skin does not prohibit from any place or station that he or she may be capable of occupying.

The Palace, where the Emperor resides, is called the Court, the seat of government. This magnificent building is adorned with all the ornaments that possibly can be explained; there are hundreds of people that inhabit it, besides the soldiers that guard. There are several of these splendid edifices in the city and vicinity. The one that I was presented in, was in a village, three miles from the city. After leaving the carriage, we entered the first ward; the usual salutation by guards was performed. As we passed through the beautiful hall, a door was opened by two colored men, in official dress, and there stood the Emperor Alexander on his throne, in royal apparel. The throne is circular, elevated two steps from the floor, and covered with scarlet velvet tasseled with gold. As I entered, the Emperor stepped forward with great politeness and condescension, and welcomed and asked me several questions; he then accompanied us to the Empress Elizabeth; she stood in her dignity, and received me in the same manner. They presented me with a gold watch, and fifty dollars in gold.

The number of colored men that filled this station was twenty; when one dies, the number is immediately made up. Mr. Prince filled the place of one that had died. They serve in turns, four at a time, except on some great occasions, when all are employed. Provision is made for the families within or without the Palace. Those without go to Court at 8 o'clock in the morning; after breakfasting, they take their station in the halls, for the purpose of opening the doors, at signal given, when the Emperor and Empress pass.

First of August we visited the burying-ground, where the people meet, as they say, to pay respect to their dead. It is a great holiday; they drink and feast on the grave stones, or as near the grave as they can come; some groan and pray, and some have music and dancing. At a funeral no one attends except the invited; after the friends arrive, a dish of rice boiled hard, with raisins, is handed round; all are to take a spoonful, with the same spoon, and out of the same dish; in the meanwhile the priest, with his clerk, performs the ceremony, perfuming the room with incense. The lid is not put on to the coffin, the corpse being laid out in his or her best dress. The torch-men (who are dressed in black garments, made to slope down to their feet, with broad brimmed hats that cover their shoulders,) form a procession, with lighted torches in their hands, bowing their heads as they pass along very gravely; then comes one more, with the lid on his head; then the hearse with the corpse, drawn by four horses, covered with black gowns down to their feet; they all move along with great solemnity. Before entering the grave-yard, the procession goes to an adjoining church, where there are many ladies, placed on benches, side by side, according to their ages; the ladies dressed as if they were going to a ball-room, displaying a most dreadful appearance. Each one has her hands crossed, and holding in one of them a pass to give to Peter, that they may enter into Heaven. At this place they light their candles, and receive their rice in the manner before mentioned. The top is then put on to the coffin, and the procession forms and repairs to the grave; the priest sanctifies the grave, then casts in dust, and the coffin is consigned to its narrow-house; then commence the yells; they drink, eat cake, black bread, and finish their rice, when the party return back to dinner, where every thing has been prepared during their absence. This is the Greek mode of burying their dead. On the birth of a child, the babe is not dressed until it is baptized; it is immersed all over in water; a stand, with an oval basin, is brought for the purpose by the clerk. The mother is presented with gifts, which are placed under her pillow. Should the babe die before this rite is performed, it is not placed with the others; but should it die having been baptized, although not more than two hours old, it is dressed and placed on the bench at church with the rest. In this manner the common people bury their dead.

When any of the Imperial family dies, they are laid in state forty days, and every thing accordingly. There is a building built expressly for the Imperial families, where their remains are deposited. In the front part of it, the criminals that have rebelled against the Imperial family are placed in cells, thus combining the prison and the tomb; and in sailing by, these miserable creatures are exposed to the careless gaze of unfeeling observers.

St. Petersburg was inundated October 9th, 1824. The water rose sixteen feet in most parts of the city; many of the inhabitants were drowned. An Island between the city and Cronstradt, containing five hundred inhabitants, was inundated, and all were drowned, and great damage was done at Cronstradt. The morning of this day was fair; there was a high wind. Mr. Prince went early to the Palace, as it was his turn to serve; our children boarders were gone to school; our servant had gone of an errand. I heard a cry, and to my astonishment, when I looked out to see what was the matter, the waters covered the earth. I had not then learned the language, but I beckoned to the people to come in; the waters continued to rise until 10 o'clock, A.M. The waters were then within two inches of my window, when they ebbed and went out as fast as they had come in, leaving to our view a dreadful sight. The people who came into my house for their safety retired, and I was left alone. At four o'clock in the afternoon, there was darkness that might be felt, such as I had never experienced before. My situation was the more painful being alone, and not being able to speak. I waited until ten in the evening; I then took a lantern, and started to go to a neighbor's, whose children went to the same school with my boarders. I made my way through a long yard, over the bodies of men and beasts, and when opposite their gate I sunk; I made one grasp, and the earth gave away; I grasped again, and fortunately got hold of the leg of a horse, that had been drowned. I drew myself up covered with mire, and made my way a little further, when I was knocked down by striking against a boat, that had been washed up and left by the retiring waters; and as I had lost my lantern, I was obliged to grope my way as I could, and feeling along the walk, I at last found the door that I aimed at. My family were safe, and they accompanied me home. At 12 o'clock, Mr. Prince came home, as no one was permitted to leave the Palace till his Majesty had viewed the city. In the morning the children and the girl returned, and I went to view the pit into which I had sunk. It was large enough to hold a dozen like myself, when the earth had caved in. Had not that horse been there, I should never again seen the light of day, and no one would have known my fate. Thus, through the providence of God, I escaped from the flood and the pit.

"My helper, God, I bless thy name;
The same thy power, thy grace the same;
I midst ten thousand dangers stand,
Supported by thy guardian hand."

Should I attempt to give an account of all the holidays, it would fill volumes. The next to notice is Christmas and New Year. The first day of January a grand masquerade is given by his Majesty, at the winter Palace; forty thousand tickets are distributed; every thing is done in order; every gentleman wears a mask and cloak, and carries a lady with him. They are formed in a procession, and enter at the west gate; as they pass through, all the golden vessels and ornaments are displayed; these were back of a counter, which extends two hundred feet; there the company receive a cup of hot chocolate, and a paper of comfits, and a bun; a great many are in attendance, as a vast many persons are permitted to pass in and view the Palace, and go out at the east gate.

The 6th of January is a still greater day, for then the water is christened; a church is built on the ice, ornamented with gold and evergreens, and a row of spruce trees, extending from the door of the Palace to the church. At this time all the nobles, of different nations, make their appearance in their native costume. The Patriarch, Archbishops, and other dignitaries of the Court, have a service; then they pass through and christen the water, and make it holy; then there is a great rush of the people for this holy water. On the plane an ice hill is built, eighty feet high, where the Emperor and his Court exercise themselves.

February 10th is another holiday. Buildings are constructed on the plane for the occasion. All kinds of amusements may be found here, and all kinds of animals seen; much time and money are spent. The buildings are built in rotation. All the children of the different seminaries and institutions of education, are driven round in gilded carriages to witness the performances. After this is the great Fast, previous to the crucifixion of our Saviour. Then Christ is represented as riding into Jerusalem; branches of trees are placed in the ice, and strewed through the streets, and every performance is carried out. The Saviour is made of white marble; he is crucified and buried, and on the third day he rises, according to the Scriptures; then the cannons are fired. At the close of this forty day's Fast, they have a great Feast and Fair; all business is suspended, and the festivity and frolic continue for one week.

The first of May is another great holiday. The merchants' daughters are arranged on each side of a long mall, in the beautiful gardens, and arrayed in their best clothes, under the care of an old woman known in their families; the gentlemen walk round and observe them, and if they see one they fancy, they speak to the old woman; she takes him to the parents and introduces him; if the parties agree, they prepare for the betrothal. It is their custom to marry one of their own station. All these holidays are accounted sacred. The first year I noted them all, as I was accustomed to attend them.

May, 1825, I spent some time visiting the different towns in the vicinity of St. Petersburg. In the fall of the same year, the Emperor retired to a warmer climate for the health of the Empress Elizabeth. January, 1826, the corpse of Alexander was brought in state, and was met three miles from the city by the nobles of the Court; and they formed a procession, and the body was brought in state into the building where the Imperial family were deposited. March, of the same year, the corpse of Elizabeth was brought in the same manner. Constantine was then king of Poland, he was next heir to the throne, and was unanimously voted by the people, but refused, and resigned the crown in favor of his brother Nicholas. The day appointed the people were ordered to assemble as usual, at the ringing of the bells; they rejected Nicholas, a sign was given by the leaders that was well understood, and the people, great and small rushed to the square and cried with one voice for Constantine. The Emperor with his prime minister, and city governor, rode into the midst of them entreating them to retire, without avail, they were obliged to order the cannons fired upon the mob; it was not known when they discharged them that the Emperor and his ministers were in the crowd. He was wonderfully preserved while both his friends and their horses were killed. There was a general seizing of all classes, who were taken into custody. The scene cannot be described; the bodies of the killed and mangled were cast into the river, and the snow and ice were stained with the blood of human victims as they were obliged to drive the cannon to and fro in the midst of the crowd. The bones of these wounded who might have been cured were crushed. The cannon are very large, drawn by eight horses trained for the purpose. The scene was awful; all business was stopped. This deep plot originated, 1814, in Germany, with the Russian nobility and German, under the pretence of the Free Mason's lodge. When they returned home they increased their numbers and presented their chart to the Emperor for permission which was granted. In the year 1822, the Emperor being suspicious that all was not right took their chart from them. They carried it on in small parties, rapidly increasing, believing they would soon be able to destroy all the Imperial branches, and have a republican government. Had not this taken place undoubtedly they would have at last succeeded. So deep was the foundation of this plot laid, both males and females were engaged in it. The prison-houses were filled, and thirty of the leading men were put into solitary confinement, and twenty-six of the number died, four were burned. A stage was erected and faggots were placed underneath, each prisoner was secured by iron chains, presenting a most appalling sight to an eye-witness. A priest was in attendance to cheer their last dying moments, then fire was set to the faggots and these brave men were consumed. Others received the knout, and even the princesses and ladies of rank were imprisoned and flogged in their own habitations. Those that survived their punishment were banished to Siberia. The mode of banishment is very imposing and very heart-rending, severing them from all dear relatives and friends, for they are never permitted to take their children. When they arrive at the gate of the city, their first sight is a guard of soldiers, then wagons with provisions, then the noblemen in their banished apparel guarded, then each side conveyances for the females, then ladies in order guarded by soldiers.

Preparations were now being made for the coronation of the new Emperor and Empress. This took place September, 1826, in Moscow, 555 miles south-east from St. Petersburg. All persons engaged in the court were sent beforehand, in order to prepare for the coming event. After his majesty's laws were read as usual on such occasions, those who wished to remain in his service did so, and those who did not were discharged.

After the coronation the Emperor and his court returned to St. Petersburg. June, 1827, war was declared between Russia and Turkey. They had several battles with varied success. The Russians surrounded and laid siege to Constantinople. The Sultan of Turkey sued for peace, and a treaty was at last signed and peace was proclaimed in 1829. In March, of the same year, war was declared with Poland. 1831, the cholera, that malignant disease, made its appearance in Austria, from thence to little Russia, making great ravages, thousands of people falling a prey. It then began to rage in St. Petersburg, carrying off 9255. This disease first appeared in Madagascar, 1814, there most of the inhabitants died. It is called the plague that God sent among the people of Israel and other nations for centuries back. Much might be said of this dreadful disease and others that are but little known in this country. God often visits nations, families, and persons, with judgments as well as mercies.

The present Emperor and Empress are courteous and affable. The Empress would often send for the ladies of the court at 8 o'clock in the evening to sup with her, when they arrive at court they form a procession and she takes the lead. On entering the hall, the band strikes up; there are two long tables on each side, and in the midst circular tables for the Imperial family. The tables are spread apparently with every variety of eatable and deserts, but every thing is artificial, presenting a novel appearance. When the company are seated, the Emperor and Empress walk around the tables and shake hands with each individual as they pass. The prisoners of war who are nobles, are seated by themselves with their faces veiled. There is a tender or waiter to each person, with two plates, one with soup and the other with something else. After a variety of courses, in one hour they are dismissed by the band. They then retire to another part of the palace to attend a ball or theatrical amusements. At the Empress's command they are dismissed. She carries power and dignity in her countenance well adapted to her station. And after her late amusements at night she would be out at an early hour in the morning visiting the abodes of the distressed, dressed in as common apparel as any one here, either walking or riding in a common sleigh. At her return she would call for her children, take them in her arms and talk to them. "She riseth while it is yet night and giveth meat to her household and a portion to her maidens, she stretcheth out her hands to the poor, yea, she reacheth out her hands to the needy; she is not afraid of the snow for all her household are clothed in scarlet." Then she would go to the cabinet of his Majesty; there she would write and advise with him.

The Russian ladies follow the fashions of the French and English. Their religion is after the Greek church. There are no seats in their churches; they stand, bow, and kneel, during the service. The principal church is on the Main street. There are the statues of the great commanders that have conquered in battle. They are clad in brass, with flags in their hands, and all their ancient implements of war are deposited there. The altar is surrounded by statues of the Virgin Mary and the twelve apostles. When Russia is at war and her armies are about to engage in battle, it is here that the Emperor and his family and court, come to pray for victory over the enemy. The day they engaged in battle against the Poles, the Empress Dowager took her death; she was embalmed and laid in state six weeks in the hall of the winter palace. I went a number of times to see her, and the people pay her homage, and kiss the hands of that lump of clay. All religion is tolerated, but the native Russians are subject to the Greek Church. There are a number of institution in St. Petersburg where children of all classes have the privilege of instruction. The sailors' and soldiers' boys enter the corps at the age of seven, and are educated for that purpose. The girls remain in the barracks with their parents, or go to some institutions where they are instructed in all the branches of female education. There are other establishments, where the higher classes send their children.

There is another spacious building called the Market, half a mile square, where all kinds of articles may be bought. Between the Market and the church there is a block of buildings where silver articles of all kinds are to be purchased. These stores present a very superb appearance and are visited by every foreigner that comes into the place. Besides these buildings, Main Street is lined with elegant buildings with projecting windows, to the extent of twelve miles. Nearly at the termination of the street there is a spacious building of stone which encloses the Taberisey Garden, so called from its having every kind of tree, shrub, flower and fruit, of the known world, which flourish alike in winter as in summer. There is an extensive Frozen Market which forms a square as large as Boston Common. This space of ground is covered with counters, on which may be purchased every variety of eatable, such as frozen fish, fowl, and meats of every description, besides every other article of commerce which will bear the extreme cold of a St. Petersburg winter. This city was founded by Peter the Great, and built upon a bog which was occupied by a few fishermen's huts, and belonged to the Finns. It is situated at the extremity of the Gulf of Finland, and is built partly on the main land and partly on several small islands. The foundation of the city is extremely marshy, which subjects it to frequent inundations. For this reason there are canals which are cut through the streets, very beautifully laid out, faced with granite, railed with iron chains nubbed with brass, with bridges to cross from one street to the other. The city houses are built of stone and brick, and twice the thickness of American houses. They are heated by Peaches, of similar construction to our furnaces; the outside of which is faced with China tiles, presenting a very beautiful appearance. The village houses are built of logs corked with oakum, where the peasants reside. This class of people till the land, most of them are slaves and are very degraded. The rich own the poor, but they are not suffered to separate families or sell them off the soil. All are subject to the Emperor, and no nobleman can leave without his permission. The mode of travelling is principally by stages which are built something like our omnibusses, with settees upon the top railed and guarded by soldiers, for the purpose of protecting the travellers from the attacks of wild beasts. The common language is a mixture of Sclavonian and Polish. The nobility make use of the modern Greek, French, and English. I learned the languages in six months, so as to be able to attend to my business, and also made some proficiency in the French. My time was taken up in domestic affairs; I took two children to board the third week after commencing housekeeping, and increased their numbers. The baby linen making and children's garments were in great demand. I started a business in these articles and took a journeywoman and apprentices. The present Empress is a very active one, and inquired of me respecting my business and gave me much encouragement by purchasing of me garments for herself and children, handsomely wrought in French and English styles, and many of the nobility also followed her example. It was to me a great blessing that we had the means of Grace afforded us. The Rev. Richard Kenell, was the Protestant pastor. We had service twice every Sabbath and evening prayer meetings, also a female society, so that I was occupied at all times.

At the time of the inundation, the Bibles and other books belonging to the society were injured. But Mr. Kenell took the liberty to purchase at full price and sell at an advance. In order that the poor might have them, we all agreed to labor for that purpose; I often visited the matron of the

Empress' children, and encouraged by her I took some to the Palace, and by this means disposed of many at head quarters. Other friends without the court continued to labor until hundreds and thousands were disposed of. The old Bishop finding his religion was in danger sent a petition to the Emperor that all who were found distributing Bibles and Tracts should be punished severely. Many were taken and imprisoned, two devoted young men were banished; thus the righteous were punished, while evil practices were not forbidden, for there the sin of licentiousness is very common.

I have mentioned that the climate did not agree with me; in winter my lungs were much affected; it was the advice of the best physicians that I had better not remain in Russia during another cold season. However painful it was to me to return without my husband, yet life seemed desirable, and he flattered me and himself that he should soon follow. It is difficult for any one in the Emperor's employment to leave when they please. Mr. Prince thought it best for me to return to my native country while he remained two years longer to accumulate a little property and then return—but death took him away. I left St. Petersburg, August 14th, 1833, having been absent about nine years and six months. On the 17th I sailed from Cronstradt for New York. Arrived at Elsinore the 25th. Tuesday 29, left. September the 2nd., laid to in a gale. September 18th, made Plymouth, Old England. 19th sailed. Arrived in New York Oct. 10th, left there Tuesday 18th, arrived in Boston the 23d. Sabbath Nov. the 9th, I had the privilege of attending service in the old place of worship. On this day I also had the pleasure of meeting with an old friend of my grandfather, nearly one hundred years of age. I found things much changed; my mother and sister Silvia died in 1827, (that I was aware of.) The Rev. T. Paul was dead and many of my old friends were gone to their long home. The old church and society was in much confusion; I attempted to worship with them but it was in vain. The voyage was of great benefit to me. By the advice of friends I applied to a Mrs. Mott, a female physician in the city, that helped me much. I am indebted to God for his great goodness in guiding my youthful steps; my mind was directed to my fellow brethren whose circumstances were similar to my own. I found many a poor little orphan destitute and afflicted, and on account of color shut out from all the asylums for poor children. At this my heart was moved, and proposed to my friends the necessity of a home for such, where they might be sheltered from the contaminating evils that beset their path.

For this purpose I called a meeting of the people and laid before them my plan: as I had had the privilege of assisting in forming an Asylum for such a purpose in St. Petersburg, I thought it would be well to establish one on the same principles, not knowing that any person had had a thought of any thing of the kind. We commenced with eight children. I gave three months of my time. A board was formed of seven females, with a committee of twelve gentlemen of standing, to superintend. At the end of three months the committee was dispensed with, and for want of funds our society soon fell through.

I passed my time in different occupations and making arrangements for the return of my husband, but death took him from me. I made my home at the Rev. J. W. Holman's, a Free Will Baptist, until I sailed for Jamaica. There had been an Anti-Slavery Society established by W. L. Garrison, Knapp, and other philanthropists of the day. Their design was the amelioration of the nominally free colored people of these States, and the emancipation of the slaves in other States. These meetings I attended with much pleasure until a contention broke out among themselves; there has been a great change in some things, but much remains to be done; possibly I may not see so clearly as some, for the weight of prejudice has again oppressed me, and were it not for the promises of God one's heart would fail, for *He* made man in his own image, in the image of God, created he him, male and female, that they should have dominion over the fish of the sea, the fowl of the air, and the beast of the field, &c. This power did God give man, that thus far should he go and no farther; but man has disobeyed his maker and become vain in his imagination and their foolish hearts are darkened. We gather from this, that God has in all ages of the world punished every nation and people for their sins. The sins of my beloved country are not hid from his notice; his all seeing eye sees and knows the secrets of all hearts; the angels that kept not their first estate but left their own habitations, he hath reserved in everlasting chains unto the great day.

My mind, after the emancipation in the West Indies, was bent upon going to Jamaica. A field of usefulness seemed spread out before me. While I was thinking about it, the Rev. Mr. Ingraham, who had spent seven years there, arrived in the city. He lectured in the city at the Marlboro' Chapel, on the results arising from the emancipation at the British Islands. He knew much about them, he had a station at a mountain near Kingston, and was very desirous to have persons go there to labor. He wished some one to go with him to his station. He called on me with the Rev. Mr. Colyer, to persuade me to go. I told him it was my intention to go if I could make myself useful, but that I was sensible that I was very limited in education. He told me that the moral condition of the people was very bad, and needed labor aside from any thing else.

I left America, November 16th, 1840, in the ship Scion, Captain Mansfield, bound for Jamaica, freighted with ice and machinery for the silk factory. There were on board a number of handicrafts-men and other passengers. We sailed on Monday afternoon, from Charlestown, Massachusetts. It rained continually until Saturday. Sunday the 23d, was a fine day. Mr. De Grass, a young colored clergyman, was invited to perform divine service which he did with much propriety; he spoke of the dangers we had escaped and the importance of being prepared to meet our God, (he died of fever about three weeks after arriving at Jamaica,) some who were able to attend came on deck and listened to him with respect, while others seemed to look on in derision; these spent the afternoon and evening in card-playing. About twelve at night a storm commenced; on Monday were in great peril; the storm continued until Friday the 27th. On that day a sail was seen at some distance making towards us, the captain judging her to be a piratical vessel ordered the women and children below, and the men to prepare for action. The pirates were not inclined to hazard an engagement; when they saw the deck filled with armed men they left us. Thus were we preserved from the storm and from the enemy. Sabbath, 29th, divine service, our attention was directed to the goodness of God, in sparing us.

Monday, and we mortals are still alive. Tuesday, thus far the Lord has led us on. Wednesday, thus far his power prolongs our days. Thursday, December 3d, to-day made Turks Island. Friday, this day had a view of Hayti, its lofty mountains presented a sublime prospect. Saturday, we had a glance at Cuba. Sunday, December 6th, at six o'clock in the evening, dropped anchor at St. Anne Harbor, Jamaica. We blessed the Lord for his goodness in sparing us to see the place of our destination; and here I will mention my object in visiting Jamaica. I hoped that I might aid, in some small degree, to raise up and encourage the emancipated inhabitants, and teach the young children to read and work, to fear God, and put their trust in the Saviour. Mr. Whitmarsh and his friend came on board and welcomed us. On Tuesday we went on shore to see the place and the people; my intention had been to go directly to Kingston, but the people urged me to stay with them and I thought it my duty to comply, and wrote to Mr. Ingraham to that effect. I went first to see the minister, Mr. Abbott, I thought as he was out, I had better wait his return. The people promised to pay me for my services, or send me to Kingston. When Mr. Abbot returned he made me an offer, which I readily accepted. As I lodged in the house of one of the class-leaders I attended her class a few times, and when I learned the method, I stopped. She then commenced her authority and gave me to understand if I did not comply I should not have any pay from that society. I spoke to her of the necessity of being born of the spirit of God before we become members of the church of Christ, and told her I was sorry to see the people blinded in such a way.

She was very angry with me and soon accomplished her end by complaining of me to the minister; and I soon found I was to be dismissed unless I would yield obedience to this class-leader. I told the minister that I did not come there to be guided by a poor foolish woman. He then told me that I had spoken something about the necessity of moral conduct in church members. I told him I had, and in my opinion, I was sorry to see it so much neglected. He replied, that he hoped I would not express myself so except to him; they have the gospel, he continued, and let them into the church. I do not approve of women societies; they destroy the world's convention; the American women have too many of them. I talked with him an hour. He paid me for the time I had been there. I continued with the same opinion that something must be done for the elevation of the children, and it is for that I labor. I am sorry to say the meeting house is more like a play house than a place of worship. The pulpit stands about the middle of the building, behind are about six hundred children that belong to the society; there they are placed for Sabbath School, and there they remain until service is over, playing most of the time. The house is crowded with the aged and the young, the greater part of them barefooted. Some have on bonnets, but most of the women wear straw hats such as our countrymen wear.

I gave several Bibles away, not knowing that I was hurting the minister's sale, the people buy them of him at a great advance. I gave up my school at St. Ann, the 18th of March. I took the fever and was obliged to remain until the 7th of April. The people of St. Ann fulfilled their promise which they made to induce me to stop with them. On the 11th of April I arrived at Kingston, and was conducted to the Mico

Institution, where Mr. Ingraham directed me to find him; he had lost his pulpit and his school, but Mr. Venning, the teacher, kindly received me. I remained there longer than I expected; the next morning he kindly sent one of the young men with me to the packet for my baggage. I then called on the American Consul, he told me he was very glad to see me for such a purpose as I had in view in visiting Jamaica, but he said it was a folly for the Americans to come to the Island to better their condition; he said they came to him every day praying him to send them home.

He likewise mentioned to me the great mortality among the emigrants. The same day I saw the Rev. Mr. J. S. Beadslee, one of our missionaries, who wished me to accompany him forty miles into the interior of the country.

On May the 18th, I attended the Baptist Missionary meeting, in Queen Street Chapel; the house was crowded. Several ministers spoke of the importance of sending the gospel to Africa; they complimented the congregation on their liberality the last year, having given one hundred pounds sterling; they hoped this year they would give five hundred pounds, as there were five thousand members at the present time. There was but one colored minister on the platform. It is generally the policy of these missionaries to have the sanction of colored ministers, to all their assessments and taxes. The colored people give more readily, and are less suspicious of imposition, if one from themselves recommends the measure; this the missionaries understand very well, and know how to take advantage of it. On the 22d and 23d of June, the colored Baptists held their missionary meeting, the number of ministers colored and mulattoes was 18, the colored magistrates were present. The resolutions that were offered were unanimously accepted, and every thing was done in love and harmony. After taking up a contribution they concluded with song and prayer, and returned home saying jocosely, "they would turn macroon hunters."

Mack is the name of a small coin in circulation at Jamaica. I called, on my return, at the market and counted the different stalls. For vegetables and poultry 196, all numbered and under cover; beside 70 on the ground; these are all attended by colored women. The market is conveniently arranged, as they can close the gates and leave all safe. There are nineteen stalls for fresh fish, eighteen for pork, thirty for beef, eighteen for turtle. These are all regular built markets, and are kept by colored men and women. These are all in one place. Others also may be found, as with us, all over the city. Thus it may be hoped they are not the stupid set of beings they have been called; here *surely we see industry*; they are enterprising and quick in their perceptions, determined to possess themselves, and to possess property besides, and quite able to take care of themselves. They wished to know why I was so inquisitive about them, I told them we had heard in America that you are lazy, and that emancipation has been of no benefit to you; I wish to inform myself of the truth respecting you, and give a true account on my return. Am I right? More than two hundred people were around me listening to what I said.

They thanked me heartily, I gave them some tracts, and told them if it so pleased God I would come back to them and bring them some more books, and try what could be done with some of the poor children to make them better. I then left them and went to the East Market, where there are many of all nations. The Jews and Spanish looked at me very black. The colored people gathered around me, I gave them little books and tracts, and told them I hoped to see them again.

There are in this street upwards of a thousand young women and children, living in sin of every kind. From thence I went to the jail, where there were seventeen men, but no women. There were in the House of Correction three hundred culprits; they are taken from there, to work on plantations. I went to the Admiral's house, where the emigrants find a shelter until they can find employment, then they work and pay for their passage. Many leave their homes and come to Jamaica under the impression that they are to have their passage free, and on reaching the Island are to be found, until they can provide for themselves.

How the mistake originated, I am not able to say, but on arriving here, strangers poor and unacclimated, find the debt for passage money hard and unexpected. It is remarkable that whether fresh from Africa, or from other Islands from the South or from New England, they all feel deceived on this point. I called on many Americans and found them poor and discontented,—rueing the day they left their country, where, notwithstanding many obstacles, their parents lived and died, which they helped to conquer with their toil and blood; now shall their children stray abroad and starve in foreign lands.

There is in Jamaica an institution, established in 1836, called the Mico Institution. It is named after its founder, Madame Mico, who left a large sum of money to purchase, (or rather to ransom, the one being a Christian act, the other a sin against the Holy Ghost, who expressly forbids such traffic.) Madame Mico left this money to ransom the English who were in bondage to the Algerines; if there was any left, it was to be devoted to the instruction of the colored people in the British Isles.

Beside the Mico establishment, there are in Jamaica twenty-seven church missionary schools, where children are taught gratis. Whole number taught, 952. London Missionary Society Schools, sixteen; the number taught not ascertained. National Schools, thirty-eight. There are also the Wesleyan, Presbyterian and Moravian Schools; it is supposed there are private schools, where three or four thousand are educated in the city of Kingston, and twice the number in the street without the means of instruction. All the children and adults taught in the above named schools, are taxed £1 a year, except the English Church School, this is the most liberal. The Rev. Mr. Horton, a Baptist minister in Kingston, told me he had sent ninety children away from the Baptist school because they did not bring their money. It is sufficient to say they had it not to bring!

Most of the people of Jamaica are emancipated slaves, many of them are old, worn out and degraded. Those who are able to work, have yet many obstacles to contend with, and very little to encourage them; every advantage is taken of their ignorance; the same spirit of cruelty is opposed to them as held them for centuries in bondage; even religious teaching is bartered for their hard earnings, while they are allowed but thirty-three cents a day, and are told if they will not work for that they shall not work at all; an extraordinary price is asked of them for every thing they may wish to purchase, even their Bibles are sold to them at a large advance on the first purchase. Where are their apologists, if they are found wanting in the strict morals that Christians ought to practice? Who kindly says, forgive them when they err? "Forgive them, this is the bitter fruit of slavery." Who has integrity sufficient to hold the balance when these poor people are to be weighed? Yet their present state is blissful, compared with slavery.

Many of the farmers bring their produce twenty or thirty miles. Some have horses or ponys, but most of them bring, their burdens on their head. As I returned from St. Andrews's Mountain, where I had been sent for by a Mr. Rose, I was overtaken by a respectable looking man on horseback; we rode about ten miles in company. The story he told me of the wrongs he and his wife had endured while in slavery, are too horrible to narrate. My heart sickens when I think of it. He asked me many questions, such as where I came from? why I came to that Isle? where had I lived, &c? I told him I was sent for by one of the missionaries to help him in his school. Indeed, said he, our color need the instruction. I asked him why the colored people did not hire for themselves? We would be very glad to, he replied, but our money is taken from us so fast we cannot. Sometimes they say we must all bring £1; to raise this, we have to sell at a loss or to borrow, so that we have nothing left for ourselves; the Macroon hunters take all—this is a nickname they give the missionaries and the class-leaders—a cutting sarcasm this!

Arrived at a tavern, about a mile from Kingston, I bade the man adieu, and stopped for my guide. The inn-keeper kindly invited me in; he asked me several questions, and I asked him as many. How do the people get along, said I, since the emancipation? The negroes, he replied, will have the Island in spite of the d——. Do not you see how they live, and how much they can bear? We cannot do so. This man was an Englishman, with a large family of mulatto children. I returned with my mind fully made up what to do. Spent three weeks at the Mico establishment, and three with my colored friends from America. We thought something ought to be done for the poor girls that were destitute; they consulted with their friends, called a meeting and formed a society of forty; each agreed to pay three dollars a year and collect, and provide a house, while I came back to America to raise the money for all needful articles for the school. Here I met Mr. Ingraham for the first time; he had come from the mountains, and his health had rapidly declined; wishing to get his family home before the Lord took him away, he embarked for Baltimore, in the Orb, and I sailed for Philadelphia, July 20th, 1841, twenty-one days from Jamaica, in good health. I found there, Fitz W. Sargent's family, from Gloucester, who I lived with when a little girl; they received me very kindly, and gave donations of books and money for that object.

I met the Anti Slavery Society at Mrs. Lucretia Motts, who took great interest in the cause. I visited among the friends, and spent my time very pleasantly. August 5th, I started for New York; arrived safely, and staid with an old friend; ascertained that Mr. Ingraham's family were at Newark, at Theodore Wells. He died four days after his arrival. I was invited to Mrs. Ingraham's (his cousin's widow) to spend a week. There I met with much encouragement to labor in the cause. Missionaries were coming and going, and all seemed to be interested in my object. Saturday evening I went to the bath room, where I left my neck ribbon: returning after it, I had the misfortune to fall through an open trap door, down fifteen feet, on hard coal. I had no light with me. I dislocated my left shoulder, and was generally very much bruised; my screams brought the girl to my assistance, and by the help of God she brought me out of the cellar; it was some time before a surgeon could be procured; at last Dr. Jossleyn came to my relief, he set my shoulder. I was obliged to remain at Mrs. Ingraham's three weeks; as soon as I was able I left there for Boston. I intended to have gone by the western boat, but by mistake got on board Captain Comstock's, and was exposed on deck all night in a damp east wind, and when I arrived at the landing I could not assist myself; a sailor who saw and pitied my situation, kindly took care of me and my baggage, and on my arrival in Boston procured a carriage for me. If it had not been for his kindness I know not how I should have got along.

As soon as I was able I commenced my task of collecting funds for my Free Labor School in Jamaica. I collected in Boston and vicinity, in New York and Philadelphia, but not sufficient to make up the required sum, and I was obliged to take fifty dollars from my own purse, thinking that when I returned to Jamaica they would refund the money to me. April 15th, embarked on board the Brig Norma, of New York, for Jamaica. I arrived at Kingston May 6th, and found every thing different from what it was when I left; the people were in a state of agitation, several were hanged, and the insurrection was so great that it was found necessary to increase the army to quell it. Several had been hanged. On the very day I arrived a man was hanged for shooting a man as he passed through the street. Such was the state of things that it was not safe to be there.

A few young people met to celebrate their freedom on an open plain, where they hold their market; their former masters and mistresses envious of their happiness, conspired against them and thought to put them down by violence. This only served to increase their numbers; but the oppressors were powerful and succeeded in accomplishing their revenge, although many of them were relations. There was a rule among the slave holders, to take care of the children they have by their slaves; they select them out and place them in asylums. Those who lived with their white fathers were allowed great power over their slave mothers and her slave children; my heart was often grieved to see their conduct to their poor old grand parents. Those over twenty-one were freed in 1834, all under twenty-one, were to serve their masters till twenty-one. It is well known that at that time, the children alike with others, received twenty-five dollars a head for their relatives. Were I to tell all my eyes have seen among that people it would not be credited. It is well known that those that were freed, knowing their children were still in bondage, were not satisfied. In the year 1838, general freedom throughout the British Islands gave the death blow to the power of the master, and mothers received with joy their emancipated children; they no longer looked the picture of despair, fearing to see their mulatto son or daughter, beating or abusing their younger brothers and sisters of a darker skin. On this occasion there was an outrage committed by those who were in power. What little the poor colored people had gathered during their four years of freedom, was destroyed by violence; their fences were broken down, and their horses and hogs taken from them. Most of the mulattoes and masters are educated, many of them are very poor, some are very rich; the property is left to the oldest daughter, she divides it with her brothers and sisters; since slavery ended many of them have married; those who are poor, and mean to live in sin, make for New Orleans and other slave States; many of the planters left the Island when slavery was abolished. In June, 1841, a number of people arrived from Sierra Leone at Jamaica; these were Maroons who were banished from the Island. They were some of the original natives who inhabited the mountains, and were determined to destroy the whites. These Maroons would secrete themselves in trees, and arrest the whites as they passed along, they would pretend to guide them, when they would beat and abuse them as the whites did their slaves; the English finding themselves defeated in all their plans to subdue them, proposed to take them by craft. They made a feast in a large tavern in Kingston, and invited them to come; after they had eaten, they were invited on board three ships of war, that were all ready to set sail for Sierra Leone; they were many of them infants in their mother's arms, they were well taken care of by the English and instructed; they were removed about the year 1796—they are bright and intelligent, I saw and conversed with them; when they heard of the abolition of slavery, they sent a petition to Queen Victoria that they might return to Jamaica, which was granted. Several of them were very old when they returned; they were men and women when they left the Island, they had not forgot the injuries they had received from the hands of man, nor the mercies of God to them, nor his judgments to their enemies. Their numbers were few but their power was great; they say the Island, of right, belongs to them. Had their been a vessel in readiness I should have come back immediately, it seemed useless to attempt to establish a Manual Labor School, as the government was so unsettled that I could not be protected. Some of my former friends were gone as teachers to Africa, and some to other parts of the Island. I called on the American Consul to consult with him, he said that although such a school was much wanted, yet every thing seemed so unsettled that I had no courage to proceed. I told him there was so much excitement that I wished to leave the Island as soon as he could find me a passage, it seemed useless to spend my time there. As soon as it was known that I intended to return, a movement was made to induce me to remain. I was persuaded to try the experiment for three months, not thinking their motive was bad. Before I left the United States, I got all that was needed, within fifty dollars. The fifty dollars I supplied from my own purse, expecting they would pay me. It cost me ten dollars for freight, and twenty-five for passage money; these people that I had hoped to serve, were much taken up with the things I had brought, they thought that I had money and I was continually surrounded; the thought of color was no where exhibited, much notice was taken of me. I was invited to breakfast in one place, and to dine in another, &c. A society was organized, made up of men and women of authority. A constitution was drafted by my consent, by those who were appointed to meet at my rooms. Between the time of the adjournment they altered it to suit themselves. At the time appointed we came together with a spirit apparently becoming any body of Christians; most of them were members of Christian churches; the meeting was opened with reading the Scriptures and prayer. Then said the leader, since our dear sister has left her native land and her friends to come to us, we welcome her with our hearts and hands. She will dwell among us, and we will take care of her—Brethren think of it!, after which he sat down, and the constitution was called for. The Preamble held out all the flattery that a fool could desire; after which they commenced the articles, supposing that they could do as they thought best. The fourth article unveiled their design. As we have designed to take care of our sister, *we the undersigned will take charge of all she has brought*; the vote was called, every person rose in a moment except myself: every eye was upon me; one asked me why I did not vote, I made no answer—they put the vote again and again, I remained seated; well said the President, we can do nothing without her vote; they remained some time silent, and then broke up the meeting. The next day the Deacon called to see what the state of my mind was, and some of the women proposed that we should have another meeting. I told them no, I should do no more for them. As soon as they found they could not get the things in the way they intended, they started to plunder me; but I detected their design, and was on my guard, I disposed of the articles, and made ready to leave when an opportunity presented. A more skilful plan than this Satan never designed, but the power of God was above it. It is not surprising that this people are full of deceit and lies, this is the fruits of slavery, it makes master and slaves knaves. It is the rule where slavery exists to swell the churches with numbers, and hold out such doctrines, as *obedience to tyrants*, is a duty to God. I went with a Baptist woman to the house of a minister of the Church of England, to have her grandchild christened before it died; she told me if she did not have it christened, it would rise up in judgment against her. This poor deluded creature was a class leader in the Baptist Church, and such is the condition of most of the people: they seemed blinded to every thing but money. They are great for trade, and are united in their determination for procuring property, of which they have amassed a vast amount. Notwithstanding I had made over various articles to one of the American Missionaries, a Mr. J. S. Beadslee, of Clarendon Mountains, I also gave to others where they were needed, which receipts and letters I have in my possession. Notwithstanding all this, they made another attempt to rob me, and as a passage could not be obtained for me to return home, I was obliged to go to the Mico establishment again for safety, such was the outrage. Houses were broken open and robbed every night. I came very near being shot: there was a certain place where we placed ourselves the first of the evening. A friend came to bring us some refreshments, I had just left the window when a gun was fired through it, by one that often sat with us; this was common in the time of slavery. Previous to vessels arriving, passages were engaged. I disposed of my articles and furniture at a very small profit. On the 1st of August, Capt. A. Miner arrived, and advertised for passengers. The American Consul procured me a passage, and on the 18th of August myself and nine other passengers embarked for New York.

I might have diversified my book with more extended descriptions of Jamaica, with its tropical climate and productions, and contrasted it with Northern Russia. I hope my readers will not think that I was unmoved by all the wonders and beauties of nature, that were presented to me in various climes. Before giving an account of the voyage from Jamaica, it may prove interesting to some readers, to have a brief description of the country. With her liberty secured to her, may she now rise in prosperity, morality and religion, and become a happy people whose God is the Lord.

West Indies

A denomination under which is comprehended a large chain of islands, extending in a curve from the Florida shore on the northern peninsula of America, to the Gulf of Venezuela on the southern. These islands belong to five European powers, viz: Great Britain, Spain, France, Holland, and Denmark. An inhabitant of New England can form no idea of the climate and the productions of these islands. Many of the particulars that are here mentioned, are peculiar to them all.

The climate in all the West India Islands is nearly the same, allowing for those accidental differences which the several situations and qualities of the lands themselves produce; as they lie within the tropic of Cancer, and the sun is often almost at the meridian over their heads, they are continually subjected to a heat that would be intolerable but for the trade winds, which are so refreshing as to enable the inhabitants to attend to their various occupations, even under a noonday sun; as the night advances, a breeze begins to be perceived, which blows smartly from the land, as it were from the centre towards the sea, to all points of the compass at once. The rains make the only distinction of seasons on these islands. The trees are green the year round; they have no cold or frost; our heaviest rains are but dews comparatively; with them floods of water are poured from the clouds. About May, the periodical rains from the South may be expected. Then the tropical summer, in all its splendor, makes its appearance. The nights are calm and serene, the moon shines more brightly than in New England, as do the planets and the beautiful galaxy. From the middle of August to the end of September the heat is most oppressive, the sea breeze is interrupted, and calms warn the inhabitants of the periodical rains, which fall in torrents about the first of October.

The most considerable and valuable of the British West India Islands, lies between the 75th and the 79th degrees of west longitude from London, and between 17 and 18 north latitude; it is of an oval figure, 150 miles long from east to west, sixty miles broad in the middle, containing 4,080,000 acres. An elevated ridge, called the Blue Mountains, runs lengthwise from east to west, whence numerous rivers take their rise on both sides. The year is divided into two seasons, wet and dry. The months of July, August, and September, are called the hurricane months. The best houses are generally built low, on account of the hurricanes and earthquakes. However pleasant the sun may rise, in a moment the scene may be changed; a violent storm will suddenly arise, attended with thunder and lightning; the rain falls in torrents, and the seas and rivers rise with terrible destruction. I witnessed this awful scene in June last, at Kingston, the capital of Jamaica; the foundations of many houses were destroyed; the waters, as they rushed from the mountains, brought with them the produce of the earth, large branches of trees, together with their fruit; many persons were drowned, endeavoring to reach their homes; those who succeeded, were often obliged to travel many miles out of their usual way. Many young children, without a parent's care, were at this time destroyed. A poor old woman, speaking of these calamities to me, thus expressed herself: "Not so bad now as in the time of slavery; then God spoke very loud to *Bucker*, (the white people,) to let us go. Thank God, ever since that they give us up, we go pray, and we have it not so bad like as before." I would recommend this poor woman's remark to the fair sons and daughters of America, the land of the pilgrims, "Then God spoke very loud." May these words be engraved on the post of every door in this land of New England. God speaks very loud, and while his judgments are on the earth, may the inhabitants learn righteousness!

The mountains that intersect this island, seem composed of rocks, thrown up by frequent earthquakes or volcanoes. These rocks, though having little soil, are adorned with a great variety of beautiful trees, growing from the fissures, which are nourished by frequent rains, and flourish in perpetual spring. From these mountains flow a vast number of small rivers of pure water, which sometimes fall in cataracts, from stupendous heights; these, with the brilliant verdure of the trees, form a most delightful landscape. Ridges of smaller mountains are on each side of this great chain; on these, coffee grows in great abundance; the valleys or plains between these ridges, are level beyond what is usually found in similar situations. The highest land in the island is Blue Mountain Peak, 7150 feet above the sea. The most extensive plain is thirty miles long and five broad. Black river, in the Parish of St. Elizabeth, is the only one navigable; flat-boats bring down produce from plantations about thirty miles up the river. Along the coast, and on the plains, the weather is very hot; but in the mountains the air is pure and wholesome; the longest days in summer are about thirteen hours, and the shortest in winter about eleven. In the plains are found several salt fountains, and in the mountains, not far from Spanish

Town, is a hot bath of great medicinal virtues; this gives relief in the complaint called the dry bowels malady, which, excepting the bilious and yellow fevers, is one of the most terrible distempers of Jamaica. The general produce of this island is sugar, rum, molasses, ginger, cotton, indigo, pimento, cocoa, coffees, several kinds of woods, and medicinal drugs. Fruits are in great plenty, as oranges, lemons, shaddoks, citrons, pomegranates, pineapples, melons, pompions, guavas, and many others. Here are trees whose wood, when dry, is incorruptible; here is found the wild cinnamon tree, the mahogany, the cabbage, the palm, yielding an oil much esteemed for food and medicine. Here, too, is the soap tree, whose berries are useful in washing. The plantain is produced in Jamaica in abundance, and is one of the most agreeable and nutritious vegetables in the world: it grows about four feet in height, and the fruit grows in clusters, which is filled with a luscious sweet pulp. The Banana is very similar to the plantain, but not so sweet. The whole island is divided into three counties, Middlesex, Surry, and Cornwall, and these into six towns, twenty parishes, and twenty-seven villages.

This island was originally part of the Spanish Empire in America, but it was taken by the English in 1656. Cromwell had fitted out a squadron under Penn and Venables, to reduce the Spanish Island of Hispaniola; but there this squadron was unsuccessful, and the commanders, of their own accord, to atone for this misfortune, made a descent on Jamaica, and having arrived at St. Jago, soon compelled the whole island to surrender.

Ever since, it has been subject to the English, and the government, next to that of Ireland, is the richest in the disposal of the crown. Port Royal was formerly the capital of Jamaica; it stood upon the point of a narrow neck of land, which, towards the sea, forms part of the border of a very fine harbor of its own name. The conveniences of this harbor, which was capable of containing a thousand sail of large ships, and of such depth as to allow them to load and unload with the greatest ease, weighed so much with the inhabitants, that they chose to build their capital on this spot, although the place was a hot, dry sand, and produced none of the necessaries of life, not even fresh water. About the beginning of the year 1692, no place for its size could be compared to this town for trade, wealth, and an entire corruption of manners. In the month of June in this year, an earthquake which shook the whole island to the foundation, totally overwhelmed this city, so as to leave, in one quarter, not even the smallest vestige remaining. In two minutes the earth opened and swallowed up nine-tenths of the houses, and two thousand people. The waters gushed out from the openings of the earth, and the people lay as it were in heaps: some of them had the good fortune to catch hold of beams and rafters of houses, and were afterwards saved by boats. Several ships were cast away in the harbor, and the Swan Frigate, which lay in the Dock, was carried over the tops of sinking houses, and did not overset, but afforded a retreat to some hundreds of people, who saved their lives upon her. An officer who was in the town at that time, says the earth opened and shut very quick in some places, and he saw several people sink down to the middle, and others appeared with their heads just above ground, and were choked to death. At Savannah above a thousand acres were sunk, with the houses and people in them, the place appearing, for some time, like a lake; this was afterwards dried up, but no houses were seen. In some parts mountains were split, and at one place a plantation was removed to the distance of a mile. The inhabitants again rebuilt the city, but it was a second time, ten years after, destroyed by a great fire. The extraordinary convenience of the harbor tempted them to build it once more, and in 1722 it was laid in ruins by a hurricane, the most terrible on record.

Such repeated calamities seemed to mark out this spot as a devoted place; the inhabitants, therefore, resolved to forsake it forever, and to reside at the opposite bay, where they built Kingston, which is now the capital of the island. In going up to Kingston, we pass over a part of and between Port Royal, leaving the mountains on the left, and a small town on the right. There are many handsome houses built there, one story high, with porticos, and every convenience for those who inhabit them. Not far from Kingston stands Spanish Town, which, though at present far inferior to Kingston, was once the capital of Jamaica, and is still the seat of government.

On the 3d of October, 1780, there was a dreadful hurricane, which overwhelmed the little seaport town of Savannah, in Jamaica, and part of the adjacent country; very few houses were left standing, and a great number of lives were lost; much damage was done also, and many lives lost, in other parts of the island.

In January, 1823, a society was formed in London for mitigating and gradually abolishing slavery, throughout the British dominions, called the Anti-Slavery Society. His Royal Highness, the Duke of Gloucester, was President of the Society; in the list of Vice Presidents are the names of many of the most distinguished philanthropists of the day, and among them that of the never to be forgotten Mr. Wilberforce; as a bold champion, we see him going forward, pleading the cause of our down-trodden brethren. In the year 1834, it pleased God to break the chains from 800,000 human beings, that had been held in a state of personal slavery; and this great event was effected through the instrumentality of Clarkson, Wilberforce, and other philanthropists of the day.

The population of Jamaica is nearly 400,000; that of Kingston, the capital, 40,000. There are many places of worship of various denominations, namely, Church of England, and of Scotland, Wesleyan, the Baptist, and Roman Catholics, besides a Jewish Synagogue. These all differ from what I have seen in New England, and from those I have seen elsewhere. The Baptist hold what they call class-meetings. They have men and women, deacons and deaconesses in these churches; these hold separate class-meetings; some of these can read, and some cannot. Such are the persons who hold the office of judges, and go round and urge the people to come to the class, and after they come in twice or three times, they are considered candidates for baptism. Some pay fifty cents, and some more, for being baptized; they receive a ticket as a passport into the church, paying one mark a quarter, or more, and some less, but nothing short of ten pence, that is, two English shillings a year. They must attend their class once a week, and pay three pence a week, total twelve English shillings a year, besides the sums they pay once a month at communion, after service in the morning. On those occasions the minister retires, and the deacons examine the people, to ascertain if each one has brought a ticket; if not, they cannot commune; after this the minister returns, and performs the ceremony, then they give their money and depart. The churches are very large, holding from four to six thousand; many bring wood and other presents to their class-leader, as a token of their attachment; where there are so many communicants, these presents, and the money exacted, greatly enrich these establishments. Communicants are so ignorant of the ordinance, that they join the church merely to have a decent burial; for if they are not members, none will follow them to the grave, and no prayers will be said over them; these are borne through the streets by four men, the coffin a rough box; not so if they are church members; as soon as the news is spread that one is dying, all the class, with their leader, will assemble at the place, and join in singing hymns; this, they say, is to help the spirit up to glory; this exercise sometimes continues all night, in so loud a strain, that it is seldom that any of the people in the neighborhood are lost in sleep.

After leaving Jamaica, the vessel was tacked to a south-west course. I asked the Captain what this meant. He said he must take the current, as there was no wind. Without any ceremony, I told him it was not the case, and told the passengers that he had deceived us. There were two English men that were born on the island, that had never been on the water; before the third day passed, they asked the Captain why they had not seen Hayti. He told them they passed when they were asleep. I told them it was not true, he was steering south south-west. The passengers in the steerage got alarmed, and every one was asking the Captain what this meant. The ninth day we made land. "By——," said the Captain, "this is Key West; come, passengers, let us have a vote to run over the neck, and I will go ashore and bring aboard fruit and turtle." They all agreed but myself. He soon dropped anchor. The officers from the shore came on board and congratulated him on keeping his appointment, thus proving that my suspicions were well founded. The Captain went ashore with these men, and soon came back, called for the passengers, and asked for their vote for him to remain until the next day, saying that he could, by this delay, make five or six hundred dollars, as there had been a vessel wrecked there lately. They all agreed but myself. The vessel was soon at the side of the wharf. In one hour there were twenty slaves at work to unload her; every inducement was made to persuade me to go ashore, or set my feet on the wharf. A law had just been passed there that every free colored person coming there, should be put in custody on their going ashore; there were five colored persons on board; none dared to go ashore, however uncomfortable we might be in the vessel, or however we might desire to refresh ourselves by a change of scene. We remained at Key West four days.

September 3d we set sail for New York, at 3 o'clock in the afternoon. At 10 o'clock a gale took us, that continued thirty-six hours; my state-room was filled with water, and my baggage all upset; a woman, with her little boy, and myself, were seated on a trunk thirty-six hours, with our feet pressed against a barrel to prevent falling; the water pouring over us at every breaker. Wednesday, the 9th, the sun shone out, so that the Captain could take an observation. He found himself in great peril, near the coast of Texas. All hands were employed in pumping and bailing. On the eleventh, the New Orleans steamer came to our assistance; as we passed up the river, I was made to forget my own condition, as I looked with pity on the poor slaves, who were laboring and toiling, on either side, as far as could be seen with a glass. We soon reached the dock, and we were there on the old wreck a spectacle for observation; the whites went on shore and made themselves comfortable, while we poor blacks were obliged to remain on that broken, wet vessel. The people were very busy about me; one man asked me who I belonged to, and many other rude questions; he asked me where I was born; I told him Newburyport. "What were your parents' names?" I told him my father's name was Thomas Gardener; his countenance changed; said he, "I knew him well;" and he proved friendly to me. He appeared very kind, and offered to arrange my affairs so that I might return to New York through the States. I thought it best to decline his proposal, knowing my spirit would not suffer me to pass on, and see my fellow-creatures suffering without a rebuke. We remained four days on the wreck; the boxes that contained the sugar were taken out; the two bottom tiers were washed out clean. There were a great many people that came to see the vessel; they were astonished that she did not sink; they watched me very closely. I asked them what they wished. In the mean time, there came along a drove of colored people, fettered together in pairs by the wrist; some had weights, with long chains at their ankles, men and women, young and old. I asked them what that meant. They all were ready to answer. Said they, "these negroes have been impudent, and have stolen; some of them are free negroes from the northern ships;" "and what," I asked, "are they there for?" "For being on shore, some of them at night." I asked them who made them Lord over God's inheritance. They told me I was very foolish; they should think I had suffered enough to think of myself. I looked pretty bad, it is true; I was seated on a box, but poorly dressed; the mate had taken my clothes to a washer-woman; why he took this care, he was afraid to send the cook or steward on shore, as they were colored people. I kept still; but the other woman seemed to be in perfect despair, running up and down the deck, ringing her hands and crying, at the thought of all her clothes being destroyed; then her mind dwelt upon other things, and she seemed as if she were deranged; she took their attention for a few minutes, as she was white. Soon the washer-woman came with my clothes; they spoke to her as if she had been a dog. I looked at them with as much astonishment as if I had never heard of such a thing. I asked them if they believed there was a God. "Of course we do," they replied. "Then why not obey him?" "We do." "You do not; permit me to say there is a God, and a just one, that will bring you all to account." "For what?" "For suffering these men that have just come in to be taken out of these vessels, and that awful sight I see in the streets." "O that is nothing; I should think you would be concerned about yourself." "I am sure," I replied, "the Lord will take care of me; you cannot harm me." "No, we do not wish to; we do not want you here." Every ship that comes in, the colored men are dragged to prison. I found it necessary to be stern with them; they were very rude; if I had not been so, I know not what would have been the consequences. They went off for that day; the next day some of them came again. "Good morning," said they; "we shall watch you like the d—— until you go away; you must not say any thing to these negroes whilst you are here." "Why, then, do you talk to me, if you do not want me to say any thing to you? If you will let me alone, I will you." "Let me see your protection," they replied, "they say it is under the Russian government." I pointed them to the eighteenth chapter of Revelations and fifteenth verse: "The merchants of these things which were made rich by her, shall stand afar off, for the fear of her torment, weeping and wailing. For strong is the Lord God who judgeth her." They made no answer, but asked the Captain how soon he should get away.

On the 17th, the Captain put eight of us on board the bark H. W. Tyler, for New York; we had about a mile to walk; the Captain was in honor bound to return us our passage money, which we had paid him at Jamaica; he came without it to see if we were there, and went away saying he would soon return with it; but we saw no more of him or our money! Our bark, and a vessel loaded with slaves, were towed down the river by the same steamer; we dropped anchor at the bottom of the bay, as a storm was rising. The 18th, on Sabbath, it rained all day. Captain Tyler knocked at my door, wishing me to come out; it rained hard; the bulwork of the bark was so high I could not look over it; he placed something for me to stand on, that I might see the awful sight, which was the vessel of slaves laying at the side of our ship; the deck was full of young men, girls and children, bound to Texas for sale! Monday, the 19th, Captain Tyler demanded of us to pay him for our passage. I had but ten dollars, and was determined not to give it; he was very severe with all. I told him there were articles enough to pay him belonging to me. Those who had nothing, were obliged to go back in the steamer. Tuesday, the 20th, we set sail; the storm was not over. The 22d the gale took us; we were dismasted, and to save sinking, sixty casks of molasses were stove in, and holes cut in the bulworks to let it off; all the fowls, pigs, and fresh provisions, were lost. We were carried seventy-five miles up the bay of Mexico. The Captain was determined not to pay the steamer for carrying him back to New Orleans, and made his way the best he could.

The 3d of October we arrived again at Key West. The Captain got the bark repaired, and took on board a number of turtles, and a plenty of brandy. Friday, the 7th, set sail for New York; the Captain asked me why I did not go ashore when there in the Comet; "had you," said he, "they intended to beat you. John and Lucy Davenport, of Salem, laid down the first ten dollars towards a hundred for that person who should get you there." The Florida laws are about the same as those at New Orleans. He was very talkative; wished to know if I saw any thing of the Creole's crew while at Jamaica. I told him they were all safe, a fine set of young men and women; one dear little girl, that was taken from her mother in Virginia, I should have taken with me, if I had had the money. He said his brother owned the Creole, and some of the slaves were his. "I never owned any; I have followed the sea all my life, and can tell every port and town in your State."

October 19th, 1842, arrived at New York, and thankful was I to set my feet on land, almost famished for the want of food; we lost all of our provisions; nothing was left but sailors' beef, and that was tainted before it was salted. I went at once to those who professed to be friends, but found myself mistaken. I hardly knew what was best. I had put up at Mrs. Raweses; she did all she could to raise the twenty-five dollars that I must pay before I could take my baggage from the vessel. This seemed hard to obtain; I travelled from one to another for three days; at last I called at the Second Advent office; Mr. Nath'l Southard left his business at once, and took me to Mr. Lewis Tappan and others; they raised the money, and went with me to the ship after my baggage. It was three o'clock on Saturday afternoon when I called on Mr. Southard; the vessel and Captain belonged to Virginia, was all ready for sea, waiting for a wind; they had ransacked my things. I took from Jamaica forty dollar's worth of preserved fruits; part were lost when we were cast away in the Cornet, and some they had stolen. At eight o'clock on Saturday evening, I made out to have my things landed on the wharf; it was very dark, as it rained hard. My kind friend did not leave me until they were all safely lodged at my residence. I boarded there three weeks, thinking to come home; but it was thought best for me to wait, and see if Captain Miner came or not, hoping that I might recover my loss through him. I took a room and went to sewing, and found the people very kind.

February, 1843, the colored men that went back to New Orleans, for the want of passage money, arrived at New York, wearied out. All the white people remained there. I waited in New York until the last of July, when I started for Boston. August 1st, 1843, arrived, poor in health and poor in purse, having sacrificed both, hoping to benefit my fellow-creatures. I trust it was acceptable to God, who in his providence preserved me in perils by land and perils by sea.

> *"God moves in a mysterious way*
> *His wonders to perform;*
> *He plants his footsteps on the sea,*
> *And rides upon the storm.*

> *"Deep in unfathomable mines*
> *Of never-failing skill,*
> *He treasures up his bright designs,*
> *And works his sovereign will."*

Having lost all, I determined, by the help of God, to leave the event; some of my friends in this city sympathized with me, and others took the advantage to reproach me. But in the hands of the Lord there is a cup; the Saviour drank it to the dregs. They gather themselves together; they hide themselves; they mark my steps; they waited for my soul, but the Lord is my defence, the Holy One of Israel is my Saviour. I'll trust him for strength and defence. What things were gain to me, I counted loss for Christ, for whom I have suffered all things; and do count them nothing, that I may win Christ and be found in him, not having mine own righteousness, which is of the Lord, but that which is through the faith of Christ, that which is of God by faith, that I may know him, and the power of his resurrection, and the fellowship of his sufferings, being made conformable unto his death, strengthened with all might, according to his glorious power, unto all patience and long-suffering, with joyfulness, thinking it not strange concerning the fiery trials, as though some strange thing happened; for saith the apostle, it is better if the will of God so be that ye suffer for well doing, than for evil; they think it strange that ye run not with them to the same excess of riot, speaking evil of you. If they do these things in a green tree, what shall be done in a dry?

"I hate to walk, I hate to sit
With men of vanity and lies;
The scoffer and the hypocrite
Are the abhorrence of my eyes.

God knows their impious thoughts are vain,
And they shall feel his power;
His wrath shall pierce their souls with pain,
In some surprising hour."

The first twenty months after my arrival in the city, notwithstanding my often infirmities, I labored with much success, until I hired with and from those whom I mostly sympathized with, and shared in common the disadvantages and stigma that is heaped upon us, in this our professed Christian land. But my lot was like the man that went down from Jerusalem and fell among thieves, which stripped him of his raiment, and wounding him departed, leaving him half dead. What I did not lose when cast away, has been taken from my room where I hired. Three times I had been broken up in business, embarrassed and obliged to move, when not able to wait on myself. This has been my lot. In the midst of my afflictions, sometimes I have thought my case like that of Paul's, when cast among wild beasts. "Had not the Lord been on my side, they would have swallowed me up; but blessed be the Lord who hath not given me a prey to their teeth."

In 1848 and '49, the Lord was pleased to lay his hand upon me. Some of my friends came to my relief; but the promises of God were neither few nor small; he knows them that trust and fear him, and in his providence had reserved the good Samaritan. One of my unretired friends made my case known to the Rev. Dr. Bigelow and wife, who sought me out in my distress. I shall not soon forget the morning she came to me, with an expression of love and kindness, wishing to know my case. Mrs. Bigelow was the daughter of Captain Theodore Stanwood, of Gloucester, whom Mr. Prince sailed with as steward the first time he went to Russia. Mrs. B. is one of the kind friends I speak of, when carried to Gloucester sick, in 1814; she was then a little miss. A friend of mine lived with her mother; she used to say that Amelia would not rest, when she came from school, till she had something to bring to my mother and me. Mrs. Bigelow and family were very kind, doing all in their power to make me comfortable, and even moved me from the house of the tyrant that I then hired from, and raised me up other kind friends; and, with the blessing of God and the counsel of Dr. Grey, my health is much improved. "I am as a wonder unto many, but the Lord is my strong refuge." Underneath him is the everlasting arm of mercy; misfortune is never mournful for the soul that accepts it, for such do always see that every cloud is an angel's face; sorrow connects the soul with the invisible.

O Father, fearful indeed is this world's pilgrimage, when the soul has learned that all its sounds are echos, all its sights are shadows. But lo! a cloud opens, a face serene and hopeful looks forth and saith, "Be thou as a little child, and thus shalt thou become a seraph, and bow thyself in silent humility and pray, not that afflictions might not visit, but be willing to be purified through fire, and accept it meekly."

DIVINE CONTENTMENT

Advancement of Faith is Necessary.

All our disquietnesses do issue immediately from unbelief. It is this that raiseth the storm of discontent in the heart. Oh, set faith at work! It is the property of faith to silence our doubtings, to scatter our fears, to still the heart when the passions are up. Faith works the heart to a sweet serene composure: it is not having food and raiment, but having faith, which will make us content. Faith chides down passion; when Reason begins to swim, let Faith swim.

Quest. How doth Faith work contentment?

Answ. 1. Faith shows the soul that whatever its trials are, yet it is from the hand of a kind Father: it is indeed a bitter cup; but "shall I not drink the cup which my Father hath given me to drink?" (John xviii. 11.) It is love to my soul; God *corrects* with the same love that he *crowns* me. God is now training me up for heaven; he carves me, to make me a polished pillar, fit to stand in the heavenly mansion. These sufferings bring forth patience, humility, even the peaceable fruits of righteousness, Heb. xii. 11. And if God can bring such sweet fruit out of a sour stock, let him graft me where he please. Thus faith brings the heart to holy contentment.

2. Faith sucks the honey of contentment out of the hive of the Promise. Christ is the Vine, the promises are the clusters of grapes that grow upon this Vine; and Faith presseth the sweet vine of contentment out of these spiritual clusters of the promises. I will show you but one cluster,—The Lord will give grace and glory, and no good thing will he withhold from them that walk uprightly; (Psal. lxxxiv. 11,) here is enough for faith to live upon. The Promise is the flower out of which Faith distils the spirits and quintessence of divine contentment. In a word, Faith carries up the soul, and makes it aspire after more noble and generous delights than earth affords, and to live in the world above the world. Would you lead contented lives, live up to the height of your faith.

Breath after Assurance.

Oh, let us get the interest cleared between God and our own souls! Interest is a word much in use; a pleasing word: interest in great friends, interest-money. Oh, if there be an interest worth looking after, it is an interest between God and the soul. Labor to say with Thomas, my Lord and my God. To be without money and without friends, and without God too, (Eph. ii. 12,) is said; but he whose faith doth flourish into assurance, that can say, with St. Paul—I know in whom I have believed, (2 Tim. i. 12.) Be assured that man hath enough to give his heart contentment. When a man's debts are paid, and he can go abroad without fear of arresting, what contentment is this! Oh, let your title be cleared! if God be ours, whatever we want in the creature is infinitely made up in him. Do I want bread? I have Christ, the Bread of Life. Am I under defilement? His blood is like the trees of the sanctuary; not only for meat, but medicine, Ezek. xlvii. 12. If any thing in the world is worth laboring for, it is to get sound evidences that God is ours. If this be once cleared, what can come amiss? No matter what storms I meet with, so that I know where to put in for harbor. He that hath God to be his God, is so well contented with his condition, that he doth not much care whether he hath any thing else. To rest in a condition where a Christian cannot say God is his God, is a matter of *fear*: and if he can say so truly, and yet is not contented, is matter of *shame*. David encouraged himself in the Lord his God. Although it was sad with him, (1 Sam. xxx. 62.) Ziklag was burnt, his wives taken captive, he lost all, and had like to have lost his soldiers' hearts too—for they spake of stoning him—yet he had the ground of contentment within him, viz., an interest in God; and this was a pillar of supportment to his spirit. He that knows God is his, and that all that is in God is for his good; if this doth not satisfy, I know nothing will.

Pray for an Humble Spirit.

The humble man is the contented man: if his estate be low, his heart is lower than his estate; therefore he is contented. If his esteem is the world below, he that is little in his own eyes, will not be much troubled to be little in the eyes of others. He hath a meaner opinion of himself, than others can have of him. The humble man studies his own unworthiness; he looks upon himself as less than the least of God's mercies, (Gen. xxxii. 10,) and then a little will content him. He cries out with Paul, that he is the chief of sinners, (1 Tim. i. 15,) therefore doth not murmur, but admire: he doth not say his comforts are small, but his sins are great. He thinks it a mercy he is out of hell; therefore, is contented. He doth not go to carve out a more happy condition to himself; he knows the worst piece God cuts him is better than he deserves. A proud man is never contented; he is one that hath an high opinion of himself; therefore, under small blessings is disdainful, under small crosses impatient. The humble spirit is the contented spirit; if his cross be light, he reckons it in the inventory of his mercies; if it be heavy, yet takes it upon his knees, knowing that when his estate is bad, it is to make him the better. Where you lay humility for the foundation, contentment will be the superstructure, and Christ the topstone.

Keep a clear Conscience. 1 Tim. iii. 9.

Contentment is the *manna* that is laid up in the ark of a good conscience. Oh, take heed of indulging any sin! It is as natural for guilt to breed disquietude, as for the earth to breed worms. Sin lies like Jonah in the ship, it raises a tempest. If dust or motes be gotten into the eye, they make the eye water, and cause a soreness in it; if the eye be clear, then it is free from that soreness. If sin be gotten into the conscience, which is as the eye of the soul, then grief and disquiet breed there: but keep the eye of conscience clear, and all is well. What Solomon saith of a good stomach, I may say of a good conscience (Prov. xxvii. 7.) To the hungry soul every bitter thing is sweet; so to a good conscience every bitter thing is sweet; it can pick contentment out of the Cross. A good conscience turns the waters of Marah into wine. Would you have a quiet heart? Get a smiling conscience. I wonder not to hear Paul say, he was in every state content; when he could make that triumph—I have lived in all good conscience unto this day, Acts, xxiii. 1. When once a man's reckonings are clear, it must needs let in abundance of contentment into the heart. A good conscience can suck contentment out of the bitterest drug: under slanders—This is our rejoicing, the testimony of our conscience, 2 Cor. i. 12. In case of imprisonment, Paul had his prison-songs, and could play the sweet lesson of contentment when his feet were in the stocks, Acts xvi. 24. Augustine calls it the paradise of a good conscience. When the times are troublesome, a good conscience makes a calm: if conscience be clear, what though the days be cloudy? . . . Oh, keep conscience clear, and you shall never want contentment!

The Hiding Place

Amid this world's tumultuous noise,
For peace my soul to Jesus flies;
If I've an interest in his grace,
I want no other hiding place.

The world with all its charms is vain,
Its wealth and honors I disdain;
All its extensive aims embrace,
Can ne'er afford a hiding place.

A guilty sinful heart is mine,
Jesus, unbounded love is thine!
When I behold thy smiling face,
'Tis then I see my hiding place.

To save, if once my Lord engage,
The world may laugh, and Satan rage:
The powers of hell can ne'er erase
My name from God's own hiding place.

I'm in a wilderness below,
Lord, guide me all my journey through,
Plainly let me thy footsteps trace,
Which lead to heaven my hiding place.

Should dangers thick impede my course,
O let my soul sustain no loss;
Help me to run the Christian race,
And enter safe my hiding place.

Then with enlarged powers,
I'll triumph in redeeming love,
Eternal ages will I praise
My Lord for such a hiding place.

A Note About the Author

Nancy Prince (1799–1856) was an African American writer and businesswoman born in New England. She had a tumultuous upbringing marked by her father's untimely death and mother's multiple marriages. She helped to support her family by working odd jobs including selling berries. As a young woman, Prince met and married a man whose career took her to many foreign lands. Their travels provided unique experiences that were thoroughly documented in the book, *A Narrative of the Life and Travels of Mrs. Nancy Prince*.

A Note from the Publisher

Spanning many genres, from non-fiction essays to literature classics to children's books and lyric poetry, Mint Edition books showcase the master works of our time in a modern new package. The text is freshly typeset, is clean and easy to read, and features a new note about the author in each volume. Many books also include exclusive new introductory material. Every book boasts a striking new cover, which makes it as appropriate for collecting as it is for gift giving. Mint Edition books are only printed when a reader orders them, so natural resources are not wasted. We're proud that our books are never manufactured in excess and exist only in the exact quantity they need to be read and enjoyed.

bookfinity™

Discover more of your favorite classics with Bookfinity™.

- Track your reading with custom book lists.
- Get great book recommendations for your personalized Reader Type.
- Add reviews for your favorite books.
- AND MUCH MORE!

Visit **bookfinity.com** and take the fun Reader Type quiz to get started.

Enjoy our classic and modern companion pairings!

Classic & Modern